AF492489

10 QUALITY COMPUTER SKILLS TO YOUR RESUME BY 2023

ESSENTIAL SKILLS FOR A FUTURE CAREER

ALI JAFAR UMAR

Copyright © 2012 Ali Jafar Umar

All rights reserved.

ISBN: 9798357185990

DEDICATION

This book is dedicated to my father, Alh. Umar Saieed Dantani, and to my family members who have provided me with unending support in writing it.

CONTENTS

INTRODUCTION

Computer skills are crucial if you want to land your ideal career in this increasingly digital environment. There are ten computer skills that are essential for professional success and will enrich your life. You should learn concerning computer knowledge and how to learn them either in-person or online from this book. Consider the COVID-19 epidemic as an illustration. Many businesses, organizations, and educational institutions started implementing the concept of remote work and working from home for their staff during the lockdown. Educational institutions also changed the educational system to include online learning from home. Due to a lack of computer skills, many workers, instructors, and students struggle to even understand how to utilize computers and other technology. The majority of them will be laid off. This demonstrates how to select the relevant talents to include and the procedure for put such in a resume. Admittedly, without such necessary computer skills, people won't get hired for your ideal job. However, hiring supervisors can look right into fabricated profiles like a good exit office window. The majority of professions now demand individuals to have medium to expert computer literacy, and almost all employment presently demand at least a basic grasp of computers. This may entail becoming familiar with certain programs, tools, or gadgets. Learn about the types of computing skills that organizations often seek for within job applications in this book. Through the resume evaluation form, you may seek expert advice if you're unsure how to demonstrate your computer skills.

There are two sorts of computer skills software and hardware. You can use a computer practically if you possess hardware expertise. Understanding well how set electronics off and on is a basic hardware ability. They could also include more difficult activities like updating software, replacing components, or repairing malfunctioning equipment. Many organizations recruit qualified experts with sophisticated computer abilities for such challenging jobs. People can utilize software tools and apps more effectively if you have knowledge of software. Several software abilities may be required by businesses before hiring applicants. Because companies assume that some software expertise are known by everyone, organizations might not even list them on job postings. For instance, many companies may assume that all recruits have a fundamental understanding of file management tools like Word Processing software.

REASONS COMPUTER SKILLS ARE SO IMPORTANT

Nowadays, the majority of employment needs some utilization of computers, digital phones, or system software. Some businesses need previous computer experience or skills, while many others provide on-the-job coaching. You might be able to comprehend new applications more quickly if you've gained some experience using regularly used applications.

Organizations utilize computer apps to streamline specific processes, expedite interactions, and much more, regardless of whether you work in customer service, production, the service industry, or technology. Computer-savvy job candidates are in great demand because of the increased use of technological advances at work. Finding technology qualifications on job advertisements and describing on the resume when you meet or surpass those needs with background knowledge are two ways to demonstrate your skillset. Acquiring soft skills as a job hunter expands your pool of potential employers. When recruiting employees, most businesses check for this important talent. When looking for jobs, showing off your computer-related and software expertise on your resume shows off your proficiency. Computers are practically ubiquitous in modern culture. Computers permeate every component of your life, from the device that runs your cellphone to the email program and social networking apps. Because computer systems are so prevalent nowadays, knowing the fundamentals of how they operate but also how to employ software can help anyone become more productive in both academic and business success.

Even the most fundamental soft-skill abilities offer you a competitive edge in your profession. Again, you can complete necessary PC tasks with minimal assistance from the start of your job. You may add value to a position by becoming prepared to master corporate tools and applications by possessing a good grounding in using digital systems. By doing this, a firm may teach you fundamental ideas more quickly before exposing you to some more sophisticated or niche corporate channels.

SECTION ONE: FUNDAMENTAL COMPUTER SKILLS

In the first section of this book, I will be explaining to you in detail the fundamental, or in other words, the basic computer skills that every individual needs to acquire in order to secure a job in 2023. and how these computer skills will help you have the best resume for applying for a job.

Regardless of employment or business, several sorts of computing abilities will be required by companies. For instance, you might probably need to possess a working grasp of text editors, workbooks, mail channels, and other modern technologies when you're looking for a position as an administrative assistant. Additionally, a number of other digital skills seem to be fundamental for the majority of job seekers to possess and are widely employed throughout all professions. The following are a few of these fundamental computer applications and software to master:

- Computer Operating System: The program that enables and controls a computer's fundamental operations is known as an operating system. However, a variety of alternative operating systems, such as Windows or MacOS, are indeed the two most commonly used by businesses. It may be beneficial to spend some time learning the fundamentals of a different operating system if you are more familiar with one than the other. Such systems are frequently available on computers at your computer lab, but you are also able to pick them up at work.

- Microsoft Office Application: Your job description might benefit from having some basic familiarity with workplace computer applications. Microsoft Word, Outlook, and Excel are just a few of the communication and related tools included in office software packages. If you understand how to use these programs, you can use them to carry out tasks at work. Several of the most popular office apps are word processors, like Microsoft Word and Google Docs. These include writing tools that aid in the process of creating digital papers. Organizations usually believe that the majority of candidates are familiar with word processors. As a consequence, it's possible that a job opening won't include these applications. Spend some time learning the fundamental abilities needed to operate word processing software if you discover that you lack the knowledge. You may perhaps wish to get comfortable using these programs' most frequent functions. You may use Google Docs, an available internet software program, for practice.

- Computer Presentation Software's: Presentation abilities are important technical and soft skills. Many professions require a basic understanding of presentation software for storing and communicating ideas within and outside of an organization. You may deliver lectures using a variety of tools, such as PowerPoint, which is the most common application across all business sectors.

- Microsoft Excel and Google Spreadsheet: Excel is software that enables you to swiftly compute statistics and structure data in tables. Data management and processing may also be done using excel. Some companies might anticipate that you have a fundamental working understanding of Excel. It may be necessary for you to be proficient with sophisticated Excel capabilities if you're searching for much more skilled roles. To see if the company is searching for these talents and, if that's so, to what extent they need you to manage data in Excel, consult the job description. Spend some time training if it seems that your abilities are not sufficiently evolved. You might think about enrolling in a variety of on-campus and online courses.

- Computer Collaboration and Communication Software: Software for collaborating and communicating is widely used in enterprises to increase efficiency. You can think about including relevant skills you have on your resume if they are pertinent to the employment you are looking for. Examine the job specification in detail to figure out if you ought to add these details. Slack and Skype are popular tools in companies where employees frequently work from home.

- Computer Accounting software's: When you are seeking jobs in the business or financial fields, business software proficiency is fundamental. Financial software knowledge may come in handy if you're seeking a job with a small firm and you have to take on various jobs. Payable, billing, and perhaps other financial details may fall under this category.

SECTION TWO: COMPUTER SOCIAL MEDIA PLATFORM

In the section, you will be learning which social media platforms you need to be very familiar with that will help you land a job in 2023. As mentioned in this book's introduction, we are in the digital era. This is a time where technology plays a very important role in our day-to-day activities. Most of the social media platforms are not used as a means of communication or as marketing tools for many businesses, institutions, and organizations.

Nowadays, employers value social media expertise highly as they seek to develop and maintain their digital following. For jobs in promotion, publicity, and corporate communications, these qualities are more frequently required. For numerous of these professions, proficiency with certain social media tools, such as Salesforce, is frequently necessary. You might be able to work on small projects at your current job to develop important skills. Resume whether you're searching for a job in digital networking. Most of us use social media such as Facebook to carry on working, yet firms value employees who can interact with others online and build a profile. To demonstrate your expertise in digital networking, include information about the platforms you may use on your resume.

The main social networking sites to mention in your job marketing are as follows:

- Facebook is one of the most commonly used social media platforms, which enables many organizations to carry on their day-to-day activities. Many organizations and businesses hire social media managers to help them maintain their Facebook accounts and pages, either from home or even within the organization. Most of these roles give you the flexibility to work remotely. This is also one of the advantages that you can add to your resume in 2023 that will attract the company or recruiter to hire you, and most social media managers get paid well. Furthermore, you can manage different companies' Facebook platforms at the same time.

- The WhatsApp platform is also one of the popular platforms used by many businesses to communicate, in the form of creating groups for staff as a way of passing information in a varied sort of time. Many institutions, businesses, and companies hire an expert to help them manage their WhatsApp accounts for them in order to keep their customers or clients updated. WhatsApp also introduced a WhatsApp business account that will enable businesses and companies to carry out their activities professionally. It is also one of the tools being used nowadays by students as a form of sharing valuable information and educational materials. Being professional on the platform has so many advantages that you can use under the skills role in your resume.

- Instagram is a social networking platform that places a strong focus on images. The website went up in 2010, and Facebook eventually bought it. It is mostly a portable device with way more than one billion users per month. Similarly, to Facebook, Instagram provides alternatives for online marketing to enable businesses to contact a particular user. Additionally, Instagram provides a variety of publishing choices, such as streaming services, portfolios, posts, and images and videos.

Many companies and businesses hire social media managers to help them with sponsored ads, which help their products reach their customers. In order to make it more professional for a company to hire you as their social media manager, you need to be fluent in English or the language that your customer understands the most based on your business type and geolocation. Moreover, you also need to be more professional at content writing. The majority of the content is what attracts customers to buy your product, so if you have skills in this area and can manage multiple accounts for multiple companies remotely, a company or businesses will be willing to hire you. Having such skills will add a lot of value to your resume to get hired.

- Twitter sprang to fame as a web version that only permitted submissions of approximately 140 characters in length. They have increased that letter restriction since its introduction in 2006, but nowadays allow users to post additional types of data, such as images and video clips. Several companies and businesses now have Twitter accounts to help them reach their customers and business partners. According to various sources, Twitter is one of the most popular social media platforms, and companies and businesses use it to conduct their businesses. Twitter is a social media platform that allows news and information to reach an audience faster than any other social media platform, causing things to trend in a split second. Companies, organizations, and even politicians hire professionals to manage their Twitter accounts and pay them a high fee for just assisting them in managing the social media accounts. More companies in 2022 will post such job offers looking for professionals, but due to the low number of experts, many individuals will enjoy getting paid from multiple companies.

- Pinterest combines elements of a social networking platform with a web search. Subscribers may save items, creative concepts, and motivational pictures on their computerized posters. It's the ideal location for companies to post product photographs, creative DIY projects, recipes, and distinctive imagery. Additionally, by integrating wire links that let users post your information to respective communities, you may make the data on your website's pintable. Since its 2010 introduction, Pinterest has accumulated upwards of 440 million subscribers.

- TikTok is a relatively new social media platform. Yet it has already left a lasting impression, mostly on the social media scene. The software enables users to make quick, inventive films. Around the globe, it currently serves over 800 million active subscribers per month. Organizations may utilize it as an element of their social marketing services to showcase their inner creativity and produce online videos.

- LinkedIn, the most widely used social media platform for networking opportunities is LinkedIn. Approximately 700 million people have enrolled in the network, with roughly 300 million of them actively engaged per month. Founded in 2003, Networking enables users to publish job advertisements and get responses. Users may also upload their resumes and interact with people in their sector. In terms of advertising, B2B companies frequently find LinkedIn very helpful. Even possibilities for posting material and paying for advertisements are provided.

- YouTube isn't merely the most widely used streaming server globally. In addition, it is the most widely used web browser after Google. The business was started in 2005 and later acquired by Google. Every month, more than 2 billion users connect to YouTube. More people still access the website and view videos by creating their own accounts. In essence, YouTube can help any process reach a large audience for digital advertising. Additionally, the software allows user engagement, offers information, and allows you to embed movies on some other webpages.

- Tumblr, the variety of post styles is supported by the social networking website Tumblr. You are able to insert discussions, videos, pictures, quotations, and perhaps even audio media. Ensure that a person presently owns it; it first debuted in 2007. Recent years have seen a slight decline in the user base. The number of daily viewers is still around 1 billion. Tumbler doesn't have as many businesses as those other things like Facebook. Moreover, that might be able to distinguish companies from other overcrowded websites. Furthermore, it allows for simple content re-sharing and enables advertising.

- Flickr is a well-liked site for uploading and distributing visual content. The website, which was established in 2004, was bought by Yahoo in 2005 and is actually maintained by Site Builder. Photogs and companies who want their photographs to be published on the internet are particularly fond of it. It may also be used to locate photographs that are free to use in content. In recent history, the website has maintained some of its influence in the market. Even so, there are still around 90 billion dollars in subscriptions per month.

- Reddit seems to be a global news and online platform with a huge number of niche groups. In order to communicate with those other users, a signed user can post material and leave comments on topics. The website, which was established in 2005, now has 430 million active visitors per month. Reddit isn't very well-liked by advertising. Furthermore, there are a ton of vibrant, niche organizations that make it a desirable choice for websites trying to expand their readership. For those with an interest in interacting or understanding, there are additional subeditors devoted to marketing.

- Snapchat seems to be a social network for mobile applications. The user has the option to submit tales that are read by all of their subscribers or exchange yet another piece with pals. The software, which was established in 2011, immediately gained popularity, specifically among youthful users. Now, it's decelerating a little. Meanwhile, this social networking platform still has around 360 million daily active users globally. This app creates bookkeeping for businesses that cater to young people.

- Quora, Subscribers of Quora may post queries and receive responses on a range of subjects. It was first introduced in 2009 and currently has more than 300 million daily active users. Organizations may utilize Quora to develop their subject-matter knowledge. Also frequently ranked well in the results pages are questions posted. As a consequence, your replies could even be seen by users who do not frequently use Quora.

- Vimeo, the reputable streaming server is Vimeo. Although less popular than YouTube, it nonetheless has high-quality capabilities that are ideal for filmmakers and users who would like to share theatrical material. This platform for social networking has over 6 million subscribers.

Subscribers of Vimeo can publish and incorporate movies on other websites, though. Detailed data and statistics are also available to users to track performances.

- BixSuger, One such social media site designed exclusively for executives, businesses, and small businesses is called BizSugar. A company called Entrepreneurship Trends LLC currently owns the website, which was founded in 2007. People may exchange webpages, podcast sessions, blog entries, publications, and videos. The items they adore may be debated or voted on by other users. Upwards of 2 million entrepreneurs with small businesses access the website every month. As a consequence, it's an excellent location for information sharing, knowledge development, and B2B marketing.

- Mix is a marketplace for customized discovery. In 2018, the business bought the well-known material organizer platform. Users may tailor their newsfeed by connecting to other interpersonal sites such as Twitter. The platform had roughly 35 million monthly customers prior to the change. Not all, nevertheless, have persisted. However, this social media platform might be helpful for small companies that wish to disseminate informative or popular material.

- Medium, Long-form material may be created and shared on the Medium platform. Millions of individuals and businesses share the website's content, despite the fact that it isn't officially a social media platform. The distinction is that it doesn't have as many ancillary features as some other social media platforms to draw attention toward the objective. As a consequence, it's perfect for content producers who seem to want your ideas to stand out. Evan Williams, the founder of Twitter, created Medium in 2012. Nearly one billion people visit the website every month at this point. Organizations might utilize the website to communicate difficult concepts or conversations with a large audience.

- Digg is a blogging platform with a customized home page. This social media platform covers a wide range of subjects, including internet videos, current events, and advances in science. The website has undergone a number of changes since its founding in 2004. It continues to have 8 million users each month, despite its decreasing popularity. It may be used by corporations to manage their own internet sources or to disseminate pertinent material.

- Viber is a smartphone app that combines social networking and networking. Viber is a voice-over-IP and instantaneous chat app. The app, which was launched in 2010, currently has 270 million unique monthly visitors. With certain other logged-in users, you may leverage it to communicate via voice, video, and pictures. Like certain other chat applications, it's ideal for interacting privately with clients or business colleagues. There are many additional possibilities for chat rooms.

- WeChat is a versatile mobile way for people to communicate. Texts, voice conversations, multimedia material, and perhaps even payments may all be made. There seem to be options for both solo and group conversation. Additionally, there are approximately a billion engaged subscribers worldwide. WeChat provides accounts for legitimate businesses. Because of this, businesses may simply adopt a customer-centric approach and send out information as part of an online media advertising campaign using the services.

SECTION THREE: SKILLS IN PROGRAMMING

Programmers now play an important role in a wide range of businesses because they develop and manage essential digital tools and applications that improve the workplace by making it safer, quicker, and more intelligent. As an outcome, there are many career options in this field that provide original routes with the possibility for pleasure, progress, and higher pay.

This book provides information on many entry-level coding occupations that are in high demand, along with details on their salaries and primary duties. We will also discuss how or when to begin a job in programming, considering career outcomes like source code accelerator programs, that provide a great method for prospective programmers to swiftly and adaptably learn business principles. You aren't required to master all the programming recommended by each role, but having some familiarity with each might be quite helpful. Some jobs, including software architects and graphics designers, really shouldn't demand that you understand how to code. Therefore, even learning the fundamentals of coding might be helpful if someone desires a deep IT career. Numerous new employment possibilities will be made possible by this information.

- Website Developers: Web sites are created swiftly and simply by programmers, who also create and oversee them.

In order to develop superior experiences and accurately explain customer requirements, programmers collaborate with customers and strategists to identify a platform's core objectives and requirements. Programming expertise is often required for this procedure, especially in flexible advancements such as JavaScript, PHP, HTML, and Python. According to the US Bureau of Labor Statistics, programmers earned an average yearly salary of $80,000 in 2020, though those in industries such as marketing could earn well over $150,000. The employment outlook for developers is anticipated to remain quite strong. The US Bureau of Labor Statistics predicts 8% economic growth for the sector by 2029, particularly if internet shopping continues to grow in popularity.

- Computer Software Developers: Amongst the technical vocations with the largest increase is software engineering. As software is indeed the foundation of every technological organization, programmers assist in the creation of the apps and services that people utilize on a constant basis. In the process of designing, implementing, and debugging a new operating system more effectively, programmers must therefore collect and evaluate user demands. Programmers typically engage in computer technologies, digital assistants, or computer programs. The typical yearly salary for computer programmers was $120,000 in 2020, as determined by the Bureau of Labor Statistics, whereas the typical pay for programmers in the Florida region was $100,000, according to Higher Role. These numbers put continuous integration in a strong position to be a lucrative programming dream job in the upcoming years, especially when combined well with the company's expected 30% job increase by 2029.

- Analyst for Computer Information Security: Every company with a web strategy worries about cybersecurity. As flagged by the FBI's 2021 Online Incident Study, there were about 1 million reports of cyberattacks in 2020, which resulted in claimed losses of over $400 million, as flagged by the FBI. Data security experts are highly paid as an outcome of their increasing demands; as per the U.S. Bureau of Labor Statistics, their average yearly earnings nationwide are $130,000 and $100,000 in the Florida region. Moreover, with employment possibilities expected to rise by about 31% until 2029, cybersecurity is one of the technological jobs with the strongest growth rates.

- Computer System Analyst: Systems experts analyze a company's data network to determine if it serves the expected purposes. The position calls for both programming competence and professional skills. Although experts with commercial and IT expertise can successfully move, it is seldom a career for novices. Thus, according to Higher Role and indeed the Bureau of Labor Statistics, the typical yearly pay for computer software experts in the United States is $95,000. Inside the Florida region, it is $90,500. According to the Bureau of Labor Statistics, many specialists can earn upwards of $180,000. Potential career opportunities are also created by the need for more specialists; the Bureau of Labor Statistics predicts a 10% increase in demand for electronic systems analysts through 2029.

- Mobile application developers: For the purpose of developing applications for Apple or mobile smart applications, development services employ their understanding of popular programming. The market for mobile apps has expanded tremendously, and demand for mobile apps has remained high. It's not just because it's among the most sought-after programmer positions, but it's also a fantastic job for newcomers to software. According to the U.S. Bureau of Labor Statistics, the average salary of a mobile application developer is $75,000 per year.

SECTION FOUR: COMPUTER-AFFLICTED MARKETING SKILLS

Affiliate marketing seems to be a popular option for those looking right now. Online advertising is regarded as a successful sales promotion that offers businesses an efficient route. You must first promote the web goods to potential buyers; if they purchase the goods after hearing about you, the business will pay you a commission. To flourish in the affiliate advertising industry, a person has to possess a certain set of talents.

If you intend to increase your income from internet marketing, you need to have many areas of expertise. You need to be capable of overseeing your workforce and finances, developing advertisements for webpages, and addressing several challenges at once. Most businesses use affiliate marketing to help them sell their goods in an effective manner. Now let us look at the abilities that each good affiliate requires for paid advertising:

- Skills in Marketing and Sales: Affiliate marketers need to be skilled in sales and promotion to sell a new item. As a developer, you must draw attention to your merchandise and businesses. The majority of consumers choose to purchase a product with significant traffic. You must've been capable of marketing the item to clients by clearly outlining the advantages it offers. More than you possibly can, try to study everything that is possible about advertising. Consequently, they are really the only necessary qualifications for digital marketers. Utilize this knowledge to flourish in the network advertising industry.

- Leadership Skills: To lead their workforce, marketing needs to possess business acumen. One of the difficult things for e-commerce businesses is strategic planning; you need a particular talent to lead individuals in the proper direction. You must delegate duties to management organizations, develop your staff, ensure that they are prepared to handle problems, and maintain their motivation.

- Communication Skills: Communication is an excellent method for selling people associated items. You should be able to articulate the advantages of the things you want to sell. You must keep up a good rapport with your clients and make an effort to relate to them on an individual level. By providing superior goods and services, you must improve the experience of your customers as either an online or offline entrepreneur. The most significant upgrades develop and market close interactions with the customers.

- Data Entry Skills: Another impressive talent inside the set is big data. You will really be seeking statistics as a marketer to observe how well your advertising strategy performs in the long term. Additionally, the statistics may be utilized to determine the types of clients you are luring, when they last viewed your website, and what additional material is effective. Some statistical methods may provide the results in visual forms, such as eye-catching statistics.

- Entrepreneurial Skills: Its most essential aspect in order to succeed as an affiliate marketer is creativity. The majority of effective strategists design cutting-edge marketing initiatives and campaigns, provide their clients with engaging content, and have the capacity to forge strong brand personalities. The ability to be creative cannot be taught; rather, it must be developed through your own unique perspective. The best candidate for your career is sales promotions, unless you have strong creative skills.

- Technical Skills: You should have a foundational understanding of advertising if you intend to work as an expert in this area. You must develop your abilities to build pages, cope with a variety of problems, and establish your tracking. These are all the essential skills you need.

- Decision-making and problem-solving skills: The ability to resolve issues and make decisions is regarded as the primary competency for e-commerce businesses. You can accurately weigh your business strategy if you are skilled at challenges. Additionally, you may gain insight on how to strengthen the areas of your network marketing strategy that need work. Although advertising agencies are indeed entrepreneurial, they must select the best course of action to address their ensuing issues.

SECTION FIVE: TIPS TO MAKE A RESUME STAND OUT FOR COMPUTER LITERACY

Proficient in using computer systems refers to having above-average proficiency in using digital applications. For the majority of positions, people must possess at least rudimentary soft skills abilities in order to conduct necessary work duties like writing messages, operating cash registers, or creating paperwork utilizing Google apps. If you state on your resume that you're competent with technology, it probably implies that you understand how to manage a variety of software programs, solve small computer issues, and effectively use graphs or charts. Additionally, it may demonstrate that you have substantial familiarity with data, research, and search techniques. Becoming proficient with computing might mean various things for various jobs. When mentioning these on your resume, you should consider outlining your detailed mathematical computer capabilities to ensure you are accurately conveying your abilities.

To effectively emphasize strong computers talents on the curriculum vitae, following the phases:

- Add qualifications that are pertinent to the job ads: Instead of adding additional talents to your curriculum vitae that are just not as pertinent to the job, strive to highlight your proficiency with the three or four tech skills that were already specifically listed in the job advertisement. It is not required to submit data concerning the use of software programs or statistics unless you are looking for a position that requires those with expertise in utilizing visual arts tools and web services. It is important to simply put the most pertinent abilities on the resume as well as to customize it depending on the opportunity you seek.

- Be accurate: Because skillsets are frequently technological, it's crucial to list the precise applications you are proficient at using. Some industries need in-depth familiarity with specific software or tools, which may also include photo editing if they specialize in advertising or visual design. In these situations, it is essential to include the precise technical skills with your resumes right there in the area under Skills, so recruitment managers understand your current capabilities.

- Give specific instances: It seems to be crucial to demonstrate that you've just utilized the search online so that prospective employers will think you actually have abilities when you mention these in the curriculum vitae. This may be achieved by providing relevant instances from your job skills area where you demonstrate your abilities to finish projects or reach objectives. For example, if the resume skills section lists coding techniques like Java or C++, it should really describe when you used these specific skills in a previous position.

- Employ appropriate terminology: Starting every phrase describing digital abilities in the work experience part of the resume, including an empirical phenomenon, such phrases instantly tell recruiters, making it simpler for them to comprehend the digital talents you possess as well as how you've utilized them previously. If you are proficient with Excel, for instance, you may mention that during your previous employment you used Word and spreadsheets to capture information and make infographics.

SECTION SIX: RESUME SAMPLES FOR TECH SKILLS

Both the advanced skills and job expertise sections of your resume might include a basic computer component. Your resume's abilities part lists your search online in concise and, indeed, the expertise piece, which includes concise summaries of things like the jobs you did utilizing certain abilities, demonstrates how adept you really seem to be with software. You can provide the following aspects of computer abilities in the skills area of any resume, organized according to degree of competence:

- Beginners' skills A basic understanding of computer networks as well as how operating systems, email clients, and databases work are prerequisites for learning how to use a desktop computer.

- Intermediate skills: Mastering more complicated software programs, including such versions of Windows as Analytics and Document Sharing, requires professional computer abilities.

- Advanced skills that use the world wide web, operating systems, workbooks, and webpages to their utmost potential are examples of powerful computer abilities. They could also require some fundamental webmaster skills and a skill set.

Various sorts of technology, including software and electronics, are necessary for every career path. Each expert also possesses a distinct set of computing abilities with varied degrees of ability. Recruitment management's only goal when seeking a new job is to find the ideal match between the qualities desired and what somebody possesses. The potential employer will receive a fast return on the recruiting expense when they're able to locate somebody that possesses all of the required technical abilities since they won't really have to devote quite enough time and effort into retraining. Advertising has a variety of moving components. Your affiliates must remain current with email lists, publication dates, spec sheets, interactions, and other material. They will also require a strategy for continuing their skill learning and staying abreast of the most recent technologies and advertising strategies.

Efficiency and effectiveness Your affiliates need to follow advertising timeframes and certain other important criteria in addition to being consistent with existing publication timelines. The delayed, irregular, or untrustworthy e-commerce site might have a detrimental effect on the company's organization.

Self-motivation, Undoubtedly, one of the most important traits of webmasters and authors is their determination to complete tasks. Your affiliates must be enthusiastic about their job and remain on top of numerous standards. If they lack this motivation, you'll really have to exert extra effort trying to stimulate and inspire others. Affiliates that take on the duty of creating high-quality content might be crucial to your success. You may improve your online advertising performance by discovering these contributors and adding them to your organization.

Your resume's business overview section is found above the headers and email address. Consider labeling this section objective rather than expert review or summary. The aim phrase is a dated professional resume technique that is rarely applied in the current employment market. Your business, moreover, should consist of 1-3 phrases. This must contain your name, your position, your qualifications and expertise, and their main qualifications.

SECTION SEVEN: STEP-BY-STEP INSTRUCTIONS FOR CREATING A PROFESSIONAL COMPUTER SKILLS RESUMÉ

It's critical that you have a good basis of fundamental computing abilities if you're a good employee. The software expertise you require for your profession will differ based on your organization and the sector. Although you could start off with a basic grasp of a variety of digital abilities, dependent on the responsibilities expected of you in your area, users will probably enhance your professional skills with certain technical knowledge during your lifetime. The key to getting additional work placements is to condense the strongest elements of their resume into a section within your portfolio known as a personal overview. These components of any curriculum, which is additionally known as a job application narrative, summarize your professional background, accomplishments, and talents together into a brief sales presentation in which you serve as the target customer. If you accomplish it properly, the hiring manager will want to review the remainder of your application. You need to get started by explaining how to create a stellar career description that is going to gain you full study and also a stellar workplace.

This guide will demonstrate:

- What exactly does a business description mean?

  Before needing to read the remainder of your resumes, a competent summary offers the prospective employer an instant snapshot of your overall abilities and accomplishments. It is set amidst both your full address and somewhere at the bottom of your biography. Consider it a preview for something like the remainder of your CV.

- Why would you require a formal brief description?

  Hiring managers are insanely active; they usually must wade over scores, often even thousands, of applications in order to identify a select group of potential applicants. Due to limited time, companies cannot spare the opportunity to thoroughly review each resume. In actuality, hiring managers only devote an estimated six moments to each resume. You are aware of everything that this entails. keystrokes Managers would browse credentials rather than examine them carefully in pursuit of certain search terms that match what the organization is looking for. Whereas a good description section only contains such delicious, bite-sized statements and ideas that a recruiter can recognize at a glance, you should provide the finest application description possible.

- How do I create an overview professionally?

As previously stated, a highly qualified description must inspire a hiring manager to peruse the remainder of the resume. If it succeeds in achieving that, its goal has been achieved. This seems to be quicker said than done, though, since it may be challenging to condense the most interesting aspects of your job into a review of 3-5 headings and subheadings. Fortunately, there are a few techniques you can use to write an effective job description.

The follow guide to add:

- ❖ Your resume should be written last. Until you've completed writing some other components of the resume, it becomes fairly simple. Simply decide on the most amazing statistics and information to include.

- ❖ Create it with a particular job vacancy in mind. Start well with the scope of work that prompted your application. Rephrase it attentively and highlight its most crucial phrases. The following are the words or expressions that most accurately define a given job role, relevant abilities, and indeed, the ideal applicant. Whenever you start writing, consider how it relates to your particular knowledge and activities. But you'll also benefit from a higher probability of passing via the standby technologies used by businesses if you do it this way.

❖ Your job description should really be listed within the first few sentences. Remember to provide the total number of years of expertise. You need to show your professionalism right away. It's likewise possible that it's written in bold.

SECTION 8: THE STRUGGLE OF WRITING YOUR RESUME

Given that you currently understand the fundamentals of creating a resume conclusion, the following samples may serve as a guide for yourself.

How to proceed if you lack any real-world skills?

Four or more years of expertise in the area is offered by a successful and enthusiastic service representative. I am anxious to become a member of the Techier team and help its expansion. In this prior position, I was able to create a calm and pleasant environment for consumers, which resulted in 95% satisfaction ratings on consumer feedback and 30% better revenue than the industry standard.

What exactly are the real purposes and characteristics of a job?

To start with, it is indeed not identical to a job description. They are similar in a number of ways, although they all have multiple functions. The resume goal appears near the beginning of the description, much like a work history summary. However, it generally has one to two paragraphs. The major distinction is that it describes your desired objectives rather than previous past successes. Whereas a portfolio goal may still not aid hiring executives in determining how well you're equipped to address their business's issues, it just might assist you in diverting their focus aside from their lack of skills. Having said so, resume goals are very archaic and need to be included in the final option if any are included.

Explanations of expert briefs written by true specialists

Whether you have five to ten decades of working experience, you will undoubtedly have a large record of achievements in your line of work. Highlighting the most noteworthy among them in your credentials statement is the best course of action. Rewrite this job description attentively and make note of any qualifications you now have.

SECTION NINE: FINALLY, SOME ADVICE

The majority of the information you require to create a successful job description has already been covered. Below are just a few last suggestions that didn't belong in this guidebook.

1. Insist on past success. Don't only highlight your abilities; also include your prior successes. For instance, saying that you've had pieces featured in Fortune magazine, for instance, has a lot greater effect than just stating that you're a good author.

2. Keep it organized. Consider it directly from a copywriter who has written professionally: paragraphs are a blessing when it is necessary to concisely format your material. These will organically divide your resume description into distinct, major groupings, as well as improve the way it looks and reads. Additionally, be certain to emphasize your existing work position.

3. "Brief and concise" The length of your expertise description should also not exceed five brief phrases. The lengthy description kind of negates the motive for providing one whatsoever. You shouldn't just throw stuff in. Being precise is essential.

4. You should understand it carefully. Whenever you're done, review the description as if you were a recruiting boss and ask yourself, "Why would they employ you?"

SECTION TEN: MOST COMMONLY ASKED QUESTIONS

Despite being obliged to read the remainder of your resumes, the competent description offers the potential employer a brief picture of your abilities and accomplishments. It is set amidst your personal information, somewhere at the beginning of the curriculum vitae. Consider this a preview of the rest of your curriculum vitae.

What should go in a curriculum vitae brief overview?

Your resume should be written last. Until you've completed writing each other component of your curriculum vitae, it becomes fairly simple. Simply decide on the greatest noteworthy accomplishments and fit these within 4-5 asterisks. This will help ensure you identify yourself as a contender within the initial body paragraph.

What exactly seems to be a biography on a resume?

Your qualifications for the position are briefly summarized in your CV description. The purpose of the personal profile is to give a brief overview of the given situation, not to convince a hiring manager to contact them for the hiring process. The job application profile information, a brief listing of qualifications or traditionally held, might be a precursor to the person's illustrious previous employment.

What length is ideal for a resume brief overview?

There shouldn't be more than 4-5 clear key elements within your resume description. The brief concluding text that mentions your work description, years of work expertise, and area of specialty can alternatively serve in lieu of the initial phrase.

CONCLUSION

In this book, I fully describe the computer skills that many people need to acquire for easy hiring into the job market. Many organizations and businesses frequently ask job seekers if they have any computer skills, which will enable them to hire them even if they do not have a computer degree. All that is needed is professional skills. Basic computer abilities are now a necessity for the majority of job hopefuls across all industries, particularly for freelance work. Workers who are anticipated to complete all employment duties utilizing technology may need to travel to areas of the state with highly sophisticated proficiency. Web developers, for instance, must be capable of using computer-based software packages, editing photos, and creating visuals for webpages, whereas bookkeepers need to be able to utilize systems and figures.

ABOUT THE AUTHOR

When it comes to instructing individuals in computer skills, ALI JAFAR UMAR is a pro. With the computer skills he lectures and qualifies them in, he has assisted more than 1,000 people in finding employment. He has made a fortune with his computer abilities, and he is committed to assisting people like you in experiencing the same level of success.

He currently runs one of the most effective computer training centers (Rima Computer Training Institute, Sokoto, Nigeria). Everything in this book is drawn from actual experience, which gives it a distinctive quality.

www.ingramcontent.com/pod-product-compliance
Lightning Source LLC
Chambersburg PA
CBHW072129150726
47999CB00005B/2197